Before

a

Tabernacle

and other poems

Father Patrick O'Connor

CAMPUS PUBLISHING

First published November 1993

ISBN 1 873223 26 9

Typesetting and make-up by City Print, Galway
Printed and bound in Ireland by Leinster Leader Printing

Cover: Stained glass window in Clonfert Cathedral,
      courtesy of Bord Fáilte

Published by
Campus Publishing
26 Tirellan Heights
Galway
Ireland

Contents

Foreword

by
Father Pat Sayles

When I first met Father Paddy O'Connor I noticed his twinkling eyes, his smart step full of energy and enthusiasm, and his back as straight as a rod. He had just retired from a busy 43 years in journalism.

When I met him again in 1986, nearly 20 years later, it was clear that age had caught up with him. The body was slow and heavy as he walked supported by a stick, and his back was bent almost double. One thing, however, had not changed. The twinkle in his eyes was still there, hinting at the keen mind behind them and the even keener faith.

It was this faith, this deep vibrant faith, that underpinned all of Paddy's life, and explains his poems and other writings.

Paddy was born in Clontarf, Dublin, in 1899. He studied at Belvedere College, and University College, Dublin, before entering Dalgan Park in 1919 to join that band of Columban missionaries destined for China. However, after his ordination in June, 1923, he was appointed, perhaps surprisingly for one so young, as Editor of the American *Far East*.

After many successful years as Editor he was made president of the U.S. Catholic Press Association in 1944. Towards the end of World War II he travelled to Japan at the request of the National Catholic News Service and became their correspondent for Japan, China, Korea and Vietnam. In 1948 he went to Shanghai in China, and there with the encouragement of the Nuncio, Archbishop Riberi, he set up and directed the Hua Ming News Service.

Throughout the 1950s and '60s Paddy was a roving correspondent in East Asia where his painstaking accuracy won him the Catholic Press Association Awards in 1956 and 1964.

In 1987 I asked Paddy for a poem for the *Far East*. The poem he wrote was typical of the man. As his strength declined in later years his devotion to the Blessed Sacrament only grew stronger. The faith that shone in those twinkling eyes never faded. He would spend many hours in silent devotion in the Dalgan chapel in front of the Blessed Sacrament. He gave me his last poem *Before A Tabernacle* shortly before he died. It was his song in old age, the same song of faith that he had sung in his *Songs of Youth*. His body was bent double but his faith was unbending. It was a fitting poem with which to end his long career in journalism, because for Paddy every word he penned was for the sake of the Lord Jesus he served so faithfully.

He died on 16 July, 1987.

Dalgan Park, Co. Meath.   **Father Pat Sayles**
November, 1993   **Editor, *Far East***

Before A Tabernacle

Here dwells within a curtained box
All power that fastens and unlocks.

Here, veiled and vital, lives the light
Of truth and glory infinite.

Here is the Bread that is not bread,
By Whom immortal souls are fed.

This is the faltering pilgrim's food,
His force and final fortitude,

And here all wisdom, all replies,
Await our sore anxieties.

Here is the Heart that never faints
And fashions sinners into saints,

While burns, amid our dross and dearth,
The fire Christ came to cast on earth.

Here motionless, all slights He bears
The while He rules the Universe,

Ready to work a wondrous sign,
Should Mary plead: "They have no wine."

Out of His silence comes the word
That deep within the soul is heard.

Transfigured here, to faith not sight,
He proves His mercy and His might.

How comes He here? By what device?
By love's invention — sacrifice,

To give through wounds still open wide
The ripe fruits of His passiontide,

And though we stray, He keeps the tryst,
Our constant host, our Eucharist.

Tantum ergo sacramentum
Veneremur cernui...

My Prayer

My prayer it is that I have friends
    In the streets where the poor of Dublin live.
For hearts have there the kindliness,
    The tender grace sad days can give;
And there is seen in faces wan,
    In weary eyes, a faith-lit glow,
As in a picture I have seen
    Of some calm saint of long ago.

In Dublin town, at the evening-time,
    In many, an old, high Georgian room,
They will say the hallowed Rosary,
    or in the church's ruby gloom;
And as through thin, worn hands the beads
    Move slowly, slowly round again,
Great were my joy if I but knew
    That my poor name was thought of then.

A shield to me and a comfort sweet,
    Whatever the road that must be trod,
Would be their warm remembrances,
    For these, indeed, are the friends of God;
And men, at the end, will see among
    Those to whom Christ a crown will give,
Faces that I have often seen
    In streets where the poor of Dublin live.

Just For A Minute

I remember, when I was only four,
Mother would bring me round to the store,
And just outside of the church she'd stand,
And "Come in," she'd say, reaching down for
my hand,
  "Just for a minute."

And then when I started going to school,
She'd bring me down every day as a rule;
But first the steps of the church we'd climb
And she'd say: "We'll go in — you've always got
time —
  Just for a minute."

Then I got real big, I mean seven years old,
And I went by myself, but was always told:
"When you're passing the church don't forget
to call,
And tell Our Lord about lessons and all
  Just for a minute."

Sometimes I run the most of the way,
Or I meet some guys and we stop to play;
But I manage to squeeze out time enough
To make for the church, where I pant and puff
  Just for a minute.

And now it's a sort of habit I've got
In the evening, coming from Casey's lot,
Though it takes me out of may way a bit,

To slip into the church with my bat and mitt
   Just for a minute.

But sometimes I see some other fellow
Standing around, and I just go yellow.
I pass by the door, but a Voice from within
Seems to say, real sad: "So you wouldn't come in
   Just for a minute."

There are things inside of me, bad and good,
That nobody knows, and nobody could,
Excepting Our Lord, and I like Him to know,
And He helps, when in for a visit I go
   Just for a minute.

He finds it lonesome when nobody comes
(There are hours upon hours when nobody
                      comes),
And He's pleased when anyone passing by
Stops in (though it's only a little guy)
   Just for a minute.

I know what happens when people die,
But I won't be scared, and I'll tell you why:
When Our Lord is judging my soul, I feel
He'll remember the times I went in to kneel
   Just for a minute.

We Two

When the big people sit around on Christmas Day,
I creep along the rug and get my toys to play.
We have great fun together, though nobody can see
That the little Baby Jesus is playing there with me.

While the big people read or maybe talk about Things,
I wind up my toy train that goes around in rings;
And the little Baby Jesus, He tells me where to go,
And we're all aboard for places that just we two know.

There are places where the children haven't seen Him yet,
And homes where the mothers and the dads forget...
And rooms where there are tired people, lying sick in bed,
And houses where there isn't any money for bread.

My toy train is ready for the bright tin tracks,
I have piled up my building blocks in big, high stacks;
And I ask the Baby Jesus won't He ride my train all day
And let me build Him Christmas cribs where He can
                                                always stay.

A Letter To Santa Claus

Dear Santa Claus: "Would you let me know
If you need a helper to shovel snow,
To tend the reindeer and keep them fed,
To polish the bells and to paint the sled,
To hold your coat and to find your hat,
To think of the places your friends are at?
You've got such a lot to keep you busy
That you need some help or you'll just get dizzy.

I'd count your packages, keep them straight,
And tell you the time so you wouldn't be late.
I'd sort the things as you made your calls
So no girls would get guns and no boys would
                                        get dolls.
I'd keep you warned if guys were awake;
I'd watch for the goofs who say you're a fake;
Then I'd take my turn at driving the deer,
And in and out through the stars I'd steer.

I'd study a map of the sky's best roads
So we'd make good time with our Christmas
                                        loads;
And I'd keep the deer from putting a hoof
In a chimney stack or down through a roof.
There'd be angels riding the Christmas sky;
I'd jingle the bells as they passed us by,
And they'd tell one another, watching us whizz;
"There's Santa and that new driver of his."

And when we're through, we could park the sled
At my window at home — it's beside my bed.
We'd just hop in and I'd go to sleep;
You could stay around, and I wouldn't peep
So you'd have a chance, before going away,
To find my stocking and leave my pay.

I hope you'll employ me. I need a job;
I'd be strictly honest, I wouldn't rob.
I'm sort of young, but I'm very willing,
And I'd work real hard at a job so thrilling.
And Dad and Mum would be tickled because
Their son was working for Santa Claus.
When you're answering "Yes," please tell me,
                                        too,
If you'll let me have whiskers just like you.

The Shepherd Boy

Over the hills the shepherds hurried
    To honour their new-born King;
Seeking the manger where He lay,
    And each a gift did bring.
One had a lamb, and one had grapes,
    And one brought a woven shawl,
But there was a ragged shepherd boy
    And he brought nothing at all.

All he had was a thin tin whistle, all he could do
    was play,
And all he knew was a little tune that he whistled
    all the day.
He had no goodly gift to give, no splendid deed to do;
Would they let him play for the little Christ the only
    tune he knew?

The shepherds knocked; on creaking hinges
    The door of the stable swung.
Soft fell the light on the scene within
    From where the lantern hung.
Here was the angel's word fulfilled,
    And the shepherds cried with joy,
And each had a goodly gift for the Christ,
    Save the little shepherd boy.

All he had was a thin tin whistle, all he could do
    was play,
And all he knew was a little tune that he whistled
    all the day.

But Mary looked at him tenderly, and so did
                              Joseph too;
Perhaps they would let him play for the Child
                    the only tune he knew.

The oldest shepherd offered the lamb,
                    Another the shawl of wool,
A third the grapes, then came the fourth
                    With a jar of honey full.
Behind them all knelt the ragged boy,
                    Giftless and shy, but soon
He raised his eyes to the Child Divine
                    And started a trembling tune.

All he had was his thin tin whistle, only one tune
                              he knew,
And his fingers shook as he shyly tried to play his
                    one tune through;
But the shepherds suddenly heard with awe great
                    music rise and ring,
And roll and surge, from the whistle played for love
                    of the new-born King.

A Christmas Carol

He holds His Birthday Party,
   The Christ-Child, today;
A merrier birthday party
   Will never come your way;
There's Mary's smile to greet you,
   And heavenly music played,
And Christ Himself to love you
   And give you Living Bread.

He holds His Birthday Party,
   The Christ-Child, today;
And, oh! with gleaming treasures
   His Christmas Tree is gay:
Gifts of peace and pardon,
   Ease from blight and ban,
And a share in His high Kingdom
   For every child of man.

Here is the revelation
   Whereof true prophet sings,
And here the unearthly splendour
   That drew the dreaming kings;
But the wise must stoop to enter,
   And kings throw crowns away,
For this is a children's party
   The Christ-Child holds today.

He holds His Birthday Party,
   The Christ-Child, today;
And all the world is welcome —
But half the world's away.

And, oh! His Heart is lonely
	And He, Who loves earth's least,
Is wistful for the lost children
	Who come not to His Feast.

He holds His Birthday Party,
	The Christ-Child, today;
And far from His dear comfort
	Princes and herdsmen stray.
Ah, blessed is he who, coming,
	Can breathe at the manger-throne:
"I have come to Thy Birthday Party
	And I have not come alone."

Casey's Cake

Dressed up swell, with faces a-glow,
    Off to Casey's party we go;
All the kids in the gang will be there,
    And Casey's cake on the bill of fare.

I can feel the thumps of an elephant's jumps
    On my troubled bed all night;
Now he's looking for junk to put in his trunk —
    Gee, he'll swallow me up in a bite!
Then he takes a rest and sits on my chest;
    With a moan and a groan I awake —
Yes, punishment follows the fellow who swallows
    Six slices of Casey's cake

Cookies and doughnuts we'll see by the score,
    Ice-cream, pea-nuts and candy galore;
Help yourself, but whatever you take,
    You'll have to find room for Casey's cake.

Hear that crocodile's whoop as he loops the loop —
    He's flying around my bed,
And he roars and grunts as he practises stunts
    And nose-dives down on my head;
Oh, his jaws are wide and I try to hide,
    I shiver and shudder and quake;
I jump up with a scream — it was only a dream
    That was built upon Casey's Cake.

Rosemary Casey baked it, they say,
    She has classes in cooking 'most every day;

I wish I'd the nerve to show defiance
      To Rosemary Casey's domestic science.

There's a battle begun and I want to run,
      But my feet are glued to the ground;
If a shell should burst it would hit me first,
      And the pieces would never be found!
Then a cannon I see — it's directed at me,
      A bang makes the universe shake;
I sit up and yell that I'm hit by a shell —
      It's a fragment of Casey's cake!

If you want to travel to regions queer,
      If you want your spine to tingle with fear,
If you want the thrill of your life, just take
      (Before going to bed) some of Casey's cake.

Casey's Dog

There's a sort of a comical grin on the face
    Of Casey's dog,
Though most of the time he's in blackest disgrace,
    Is Casey's dog.
Nobody knows what the breed of him is,
And the name of rogue and a rowdy is his,
Yet there's something you like in the homely
                old phiz
    Of Casey's dog.

His character's lost (if he ever had any) —
    Casey's dog;
And some hair and front teeth, for the fights have
                been many
    Of Casey's dog.
Guns have been levelled to shoot the brute up;
He's been threatened with doses of poison to sup;
Yet somehow there's no one who'd injure that pup,
    Casey's dog.

It's agreed that the bark is much worse than the bite
    Of Casey's dog.
It begins with a howl in a blood-freezing tone,
Breaks into a yap and drops down to a moan,
Till showers of abuse, shoes and bottles are thrown
    At Casey's dog.

But he's true to his trust and he's fond of the kids,
    Is Casey's dog.
Oh, they wouldn't consider a millionaire's bids
    For Casey's dog.

When they started to school, he'd come nosing
                                  his way,
And just like the lamb, into school he would stray;
But that lamb was far simpler to deal with, I'll say,
        Than Casey's dog.

Into the house comes a robber (while sleeps
        Casey's dog).
Swiping a mitebox, the bold robber creeps
        Past Casey's dog.
Then that pup just uncurls and he lifts up his nose,
And the man gets his meaning and hastily goes,
Leaving all of the money and bits of his clothes
        With Casey's dog.

When some of us fellows grow up, there'll be war
        Over Casey's dog.
Each of the gang will be clamouring for
        Casey's dog.
At home he'll be offered his choice of a berth,
Or with missioners working all over the earth,
And wherever he goes, there'll be murder and mirth
        With Casey's dog.

Pudsy Kelly's Rosary

Oh, Pudsy Kelly's pockets are a wonder to behold;
They are packed with his possessions in variety untold.
There are pencils, buttons, marbles, bits of string, a
                              broken key,
And tangled up with everything there's Pudsy's rosary.

When Pudsy wants his rosary, he starts to tug and haul,
And from his bulging pockets odds and ends begin to fall;
Old bus-tickets, crumpled papers, sticks of chewing
                              gum you'll see,
Then trailing half a mile of string comes Pudsy's rosary!

When he settles on his pillow every night, it's underneath;
It's been broken half a dozen times — he mends it with
                              his teeth;
And every time a missioner comes round, it seems to me
That Pudsy ups and asks him if he'll bless his rosary.

He'll swap his stock of marbles, or his watch that's
                              always slow,
He'll trade his comb and mirror, and his foreign stamps
                              may go;
He may lose his scouting penknife and still light of heart
                              is he,
But he'd tear the town asunder if he lost his rosary.

When Pudsy sails for China — and I'm sure he will
                              some day —
I'll ask him for his rosary before he sails away;
And then when he's a martyr, I'll bring people in to see
My very special relic — Father Kelly's rosary!

Pudsy Kelly's Homework

When the tablecloth is folded and the dishes all are done,
You'd think a sort of evening calm at Kellys' had begun,
As Dad unfolds the paper, and Mother sits to sew,
And Pudsy starts his homework — keeping near the radio.

But Pudsy Kelly's homework is a family affair;
In half an hour there's turmoil and excitement in the air.
His Dad is deep in problems, and his Mother's
                                                helping, too:
They all get different answers and then start the
                                                    thing anew!

Pudsy asks a question when a quarter-hour has gone;
Dad can't say for certain, and by now the fun is on.
Everybody knows it, but would like to see the book,
And Pudsy's more than willing to let everybody look.

"I think I learned that once." "Oh, this is easy
                                        — where's the pen?"
"I'm positive I'm right but let me see that book again."
There are readers, spellers, civics books, on table,
                                                floor and chair,
And Pudsy phones the Caseys just to see what's
                                            happening there.

His Dad brings in the scales to work the problem out
                                                with weights,
And Pudsy says the Caseys say the answer is $\frac{5}{8}$;
While Mother wonders what the course that China's
                                                rivers go
Can ever mean for Pudsy; and he says: "You never know."

Though the contrary has often been decided and resolved,
In Pudsy Kelly's homework all the family's involved.
His Dad goes deep in problems, and his Mother's
                                        helping, too,
But they really won't be glad when they've no longer
                                        this to do!

Pudsy Kelly's Arguments

I've argued over football and I've argued over fights,
And I've argued whether elephants have poison in
their bites,
And how goldfish do their sleeping and how high my
kite has flown;
But my fiercest are the arguments I have when I'm alone.

Why did you do it, Pudsy? "Well, I had a good excuse."
What was it? "Oh, you know." *Goodnight, that's not a
bit of use!*
"Well, I never meant to do it." *You know quite well you did.*
Gee, there's Something down inside of me that's awful
hard to kid.

When you argue down at Caseys' as to whether cats
can swim,
If the other guy is winning you can walk away from him.
When the argument's inside you, though, there's nothing
you can do —
For if you try to run away, it still keeps up with you.

Why don't you do it, Pudsy? says that Something down
inside.
I say: "Get lost, I couldn't," and it says, *You never tried.*
I walk along and whistle but I hear it just the same,
And it's hinting, sort of mournful, *Pudsy Kelly isn't game!*

Delivering my papers, chopping firewood in the shed,
Or when I lie awake a while just after going to bed,
There arguments keep starting up. My own I try to hold,
But Something comes right back at me and knocks me
                                                          flat and cold.

You know the work is waiting. "So do other fellows, too.
Why can't I pass it up like them?" *They're foolish,*
                                        so are you.
"I can't give up so much that's nice." *You're yellow.*
                                        "Aw, go 'way!"
I won't. You know you're shirking — you'll be sorry too
                                        some day.

And so the argument goes on. I'm beaten to the ropes;
I thought that I could kid myself, but those were
                                        crazy hopes.
There's Something deep inside me with a terrible amount
Of evidence against me and it knocks me for the count.

You'll be happy if you do it. "But it looks too hard to do."
Don't lots of fellows do it and they're flesh and blood
                                        like you?
"I'm not going." *Oh, you aren't? So you'll miss that great*
                                        reward?
"I'll what?" *It's everlasting, promised plainly by Our Lord.*
"I'll wait a while." *That's dangerous.* This scrap will
                                        never cease.
I'm going to the seminary — anything for peace!

Pudsy Kelly's Band

The man around the corner said he'd send for the police,
And Mr. Kelly called us all disturbers of the peace;
The milkman said it sounded like steam-organs going flat,
And the Caseys swore that somebody was murdering
                                            their cat.

Hear the moan and the drone of that cast-off saxophone,
And the ukuleles getting out of hand.
And the combs and the humming and the whistling and
                                the drumming —
It's practice day for Pudsy Kelly's band.

The man who sells the papers said he heard it round
                                            the block,
And Tony Murphy's grandpa said it made him take a walk.
All the babies started crying, all the dogs began to bark,
And a boy who hates to miss a fire went racing through
                                            the park.

Hear the wail in the scale though I'm blowing like a whale,
Oh, it's more than the saxophone will stand.
Hear the jews'-harp all a-twanging, hear the jingling and
                                the banging;
It's a big day for Pudsy Kelly's band.

We tried to play "Susanna" but it can't have been so
                                            keen —
The Kellys' grandma thought it was "The Wearin' of
                                            the Green."
We hadn't any music but we didn't mind a bit;
It makes you too particular about the notes you hit.

Hear the beat of the feet as we're marching down
                                    the street,
While Pudsy twirls the baton in his hand.
Hear harmonicas that mingle with cracked tambourines
                                    that jingle;
It's a march, played by Pudsy Kelly's band.

We're going to give a concert pretty soon in Kellys' yard,
To raise some cash for missions, 'cause they find the
                                    times so hard.
Though we may be making more by doing what we
                                    did today,
We were given fifty pence — to stop that din and
                                    go away!

Hear the first sudden burst, when the racket's at its worst,
It gives a feeling glorious and grand.
Oh, it's music at its best when you're drowning all the rest
In Caseys' yard in Pudsy Kelly's band.

Pudsy Kelly's Grandma

Oh, Pudsy Kelly's grandma, she can smile the nicest way.
You can see her out on Kellys' porch 'most any sunny day
Just sitting in her rocker, watching people come and go,
And there's not a child for blocks around that Grandma
                                        doesn't know.

Pudsy Kelly's grandma cannot walk so very far,
But she'll always lead the way for kids to find the
                                        cookie jar;
If you meet a boy all crumbs and jam, it's pretty safe to say
That Pudsy Kelly's grandma has been on the job today.

She doesn't care for company, except the girls and boys —
And how she loves to have them come to tell their
                                        griefs and joys!
She vows she'd run from visitors, though sometimes
                                        we can see
Herself and Grandma Casey in the kitchen, drinking tea.

For hours she sits alone, but if you tiptoe up and stand,
You'll see her lips are moving and her rosary's in her hand;
And every afternoon she prays in church for me and you,
And for every saint and sinner from New York to
                                        Timbuctoo.

She loves to speak of Heaven and it's swell to hear her talk;
You'd think, if you were listening, that 'twas just around
                                        the block.
About the Holy Family she'll chat with such delight
You'd think They were her neighbours…and at that you
                                        might be right!

Pudsy Kelly's Future

I was looking at the funnies when Dad, he says to me:
"Hey, Pudsy!" I says, "Hey, Dad!" He says, "What are you
                                             going to be?"
I says, "Gee, Dad!" He says, "Well, son?" I says, "Jiminy
                                             gosh goodnight,
It's kinda hard to know, Dad." He says, "Hard to know
                                             is right."

Oh, there's lots of things I'd like to be — and when I'd gone
                                             to bed,
I couldn't sleep, so many plans were racing through my
                                             head.

I could see myself a fireman. Cling clang! We'll run
                                              you down!
We're off to fight the worstest fire that ever came to town,
And in next morning's paper, lo! a headline loud proclaims
How Fireman Pudsy Kelly saved the poor kids from
                                              the flames.

And still I think I'd rather have a heavenly extry tell
How Father Kelly helped to save men's souls from flames
                                              of hell!

I could see myself a cowboy, with spurs and chaps and
                                              guns;
Hi! Ride 'em, Cowboy Kelly! and my bronco bucks and
                                              runs.
We're rounding up the cattle — see me riding past the rest,
And they're cheering Pudsy Kelly! I'm the Wonder of the
                                              West.

But a priest is always rounding up lost souls that
                                              wander far,
And souls are well worth riding for, more than the
                                              cattle are.

Or see me in the movies — I'm the idol of the fans,
The sort of guy whose close-up makes the kids all clap
their hands.
Wouldn't our gang keel over when they'd read:
"The Chief at Bay,
With Pudsy Kelly Starring: See This Super-Film Today"!

But a priest is always starring in life's most thrilling play,
And he plays the very grandest part — may it be mine
some day!

Or it's midnight in Wyoming and the storm is howling
                                                    hoarse.
"Oh, who will take the air-mail through?" — Why, Kelly
                                            will, of course!
And Kelly does (that's me, you know), and the papers
                                                  tell the tale
How Pilot Pudsy Kelly flew through blizzards with the mail.

But all the glory fizzles out when a fellow flops and dies.
As a different kind of pilot, I could win a deathless prize.

"Aw, what's the use?" says I, at last. "I've known it long
                                                    enough;
I'm only trying to kid myself with all this crazy stuff.
The other things are fairly nice, but they're not the life
                                                    for me;
Yes, Pudsy Kelly, missioner, is what I want to be!"

And I said some prayers, and fell asleep, and dreamt the
                                          whole night through
Of Father Pudsy Kelly, and the work he hopes to do.

Topsy-Turvy

The mighty King Kerfoozle reigned in Topsy's ancient land,
And the slightest contradiction was a thing he couldn't
                                                    stand;
While Turvy, neighbouring nation, had a ruler who was
                                                reckoned
To be very fond of answering back: by name, Kerplunk
                                            the Second.

Now, one morning King Kerfoozle took his hat and gave
                                            an order
That if anything came up, they'd find him at the southern
                                            border;
And off he strolled along the line, inspecting dikes and
                                                fences,
Thinking about new styles in crowns and how to cut
                                            expenses.

Then across the southern border, on the Turvy side,
                                            appeared
A man out walking like himself. He knew him by his beard.
"Good morning, King Kerplunk!" he called. The monarchs
                                            came together,
And leant upon the boundary fence, and talked about the
                                                weather.

Said King Kerfoozle, pleasantly: "I think it looks like snow."
But King Kerplunk looked at the sky and said he thought
                                            not so.

"I'm positive," Kerfoozle said. He raised his voice to
                                                    smother
His neighbour's voice. They argued, till Kerplunk snapped;
                                            "You're another!"

Kerfoozle glared in fury, then turned round and sprinted
                                                        back,
And panting, called his army to prepare for the attack;
While in the realm of Turvy, King Kerplunk (as you've
                                                surmised)
Was calling out his forces; thus a war was organised.

They fought till they were sick of it. Still, neither side
                                                    had won,
And now and then they'd have a truce to see what
                                            could be done.
But just when all was fixed, if King Kerfoozle said
                                            'twould rain,
Kerplunk would contradict him, and the war was on again.

Thus the noble lands of Topsy and of Turvy did decay,
And a State of Topsy-Turvy is what's left of them today;
All because of King Kerfoozle (he who had the nasty knack
Of resenting contradiction) and Kerplunk (who answered
                                                        back).

I Wonder

Will elephants ever drive automobiles?
  I wonder.
Will centipedes ever wear shoes with high heels?
  I wonder.
Will Johnny feel pleased with himself, when he's dead,
That he lost his vocation and let his young head
Be turned with the thought of the movies instead?
  I wonder.

Will sausages tell funny jokes as they fry?
  I wonder.
Will hot sweet potatoes rain down from the sky?
  I wonder.
Will Molly be thankful, when life's course is run,
That she gave up the notion of being a nun?
Will she think she's been prudent, when all's said
                                    and done?

  I wonder.

Will cats play the banjo, will dogs get the vote?
  I wonder.
Will the meadowlark nest in the beard of the goat?
  I wonder.
Will shows that are shady and books that are bad
Lead upwards to Heaven where joy's to be had,
Or down where it's hot and eternally sad?
  I wonder.

Will lemon pie ever be made out of stones?
> *I wonder.*

Will you ever see frogs playing big saxophones?
> *I wonder.*

Will people feel glad, when their souls are laid bare,
That they came without prayerbooks to Mass just to
                                        stare
All the time, or run slow, languid hands through their
                                        hair?
> *I wonder.*

Will beetles play marbles, will cowboys ride mice?
> *I wonder.*

Will salt be like honey, will spinach taste nice?
> *I wonder.*

Will Muriel's friend, Helen's frock, Billy's car,
Tom's rank magazines, Harry's jokes below par,
Help their souls by and by, if it's hot where they are?
> *I wonder.*

Will cabbage and cows ever look just the same?
> *I wonder.*

Will squirrels sing songs from Tannhaüser's "Bohème"?
> *I wonder.*

Will a man ever profit by acts that are wrong,
Or gain by postponing a good deed too long,
And what will you do if I keep up this song?
> *I wonder.*

Cuckoo!

Bill has a little clock,
    Cuckoo!
You can hear it half a block,
    Cuckoo!
When he's slacking at his work,
When he's trying hard to shirk —
It keeps saying, with a smirk:
    Cuckoo!

If he says he hasn't time,
    Cuckoo!
Hear that pert sarcastic chime,
    Cuckoo!
If he hasn't done his stuff,
If he hasn't prayed enough,
It starts singing through his bluff:
    Cuckoo!

If he's coming home too late,
    Cuckoo!
He'll arrive to hear it state:
    Cuckoo!
At the show, till curtain fall,
He kept hearing through it all
That faint message from his wall:
    Cuckoo!

When he gets a fit of blues,
    Cuckoo!
And starts wondering "What's the use?"
    Cuckoo!

Thinks he isn't treated right,
Loses courage for the fight,
He will hear at dead of night:
    Cuckoo!

But when with all his power,
    Cuckoo!
Sixty minutes to the hour,
    Cuckoo!
He keeps hammering away,
Keen to work and pray and play,
Strange, he'll never hear it say:
    Cuckoo!

Bunkum Ballad

A fellow with plenty of dough
Had only one answer: "Oh, nough!"
    When anyone pleaded
    For cash that was needed;
And now his own funds are quite lough.

A fellow who went out to plough
Disturbed poor old Bossy the cough.
    She was fond of that field
    And no ground would she yield,
So she charged, and he sprinted —and hough!

A fellow who liked to be tough,
Whose manner was hard-boiled and grough,
    In a draw won a prize,
    And rage lit his eyes
When he found 'twas a pink powder-pough!

A squirrel sat, all the year through,
Just watching a nut as it grough.
    It ripened and fell
    In a twenty-foot well,
Crying: "Am I the nut or are yough?"

A Fool There Was
(With Apologies to Kipling)

A fool there was and he wrote some verse,
      (Even as you and I!)
Some of it tedious, some of it terse,
And the time was short and the rhymes were scarce,
Oh, it might have been better and might have been
                              worse,
      (Even as you and I!)

Oh, the rhymes we've spent and the times we've
                              spent
And the work of our head and hand
Are all to tell of a pitiful need,
But millions go by and they never will heed
And never will understand.

A fool there was and he wrote some prose:
      (Even as you and I!)
There were tight-shut hearts he would fain unclose,
But the harder he pleaded the harder they froze,
Though the fool could tell what would heal their
                              woes
      (Even as you and I!)

Oh, the reams we wrote and the dreams we wrote
And the excellent things we planned
Were all to help the hearts that were sad,
Were all for the people who thought we were mad
And they never would understand.

A fool there was and he said his say, —
       (Even as you and I!)
Some shrugged their shoulders and hurried to play,
Some listened a while and then went their way,
And the fool he wept at the end of the day —
       (Even as you and I!)

But the ways we plead and the days we plead
And the fervour we'd fain have fanned
Are all for One who never will fail
To value the deed, though it flourish or fail —
And He always will understand.

A Song For All Fools

There's this and that to celebrate,
And hallowed days are dear,
And memory keeps her secret shrines
Along the winding year;
And here's a date we well may mark,
Though not with pleasures gay;
Let each one keep with bitter zest
A feast on All Fools' Day.

The man who's sure that due respect
For all his gifts is shown,
Who's slow to see another's fault,
But quick to tell his own;
Who talks to boss and janitor
In just the same sweet way,
Let him alone — it's not his feast;
It's ours, on All Fool's Day.

It's ours, by all the chances missed,
The kind words never said,
The wistful hearts we might have helped,
The aches we caused instead,
By all the work we didn't do,
The prayers we didn't say,
By all the time we've lost — it's ours,
This feast of All Fools' Day.

For all the thoughts that made ourselves
The centres of the world,
The times when at another's deed
Disdainful lips we curled,
For all we've spent but might have saved
For souls in sad mishap —
Today let's bow our heads in shame
To take the Dunce's Cap.

For restless tongues, for clumsy hands,
For foolish fears and fuss,
May He whose word says "Suffer fools"
Pardon and bear with us;
And now against all pride and pique,
All pomp and vain pretence,
We'll make our prayer tonight, and may
The good Lord give us sense!

Our Dan

Knots in his shoestrings, dirt on his clothes,
Junk in his pockets, ink on his nose.
What in the world will he be when he grows?
        Our Boy Dan.

He pals with the mailman, chums with the cop,
Rides with the milkman, and knows every stop.
The man with the peanut-stand calls him "Old Top" —
        That's Our Dan.

Tangling his kite in your wires and your trees,
Itching to climb every wall that he sees.
Scrapes on his elbows and cuts on his knees —
        That's Our Dan.

The nonsense you heard when your telephone rang,
The football you found when your window went bang,
The blood-curdling yells as he rallied the gang —
        That's Our Dan.

Over to Casey's he's bristling with fight;
He'll be scared as a rabbit on next Sunday night,
When there's company in and he's asked to recite —
        Yes, That's Dan.

Oh, I never can tell you what I felt like
The night he was carried in — knocked off his bike,
Gosh, he sure had us frightened, the blamed little tike —
        Our Own Dan.

He'd be a wild cowboy — he said so, at least;
Now he talks of big work in the far foreign East:
And to "What will you be, Dan?" he whispers, "A pr——!"
Shucks, Our Dan!

Yes, it looks like it's coming, and I'll surely feel glad;
There are trials in the world, but thank God I'm his Dad!
Ah, to think that some day I'll serve Mass for my lad —
Our Father Dan!

The Angel of the Pearls

Now, the angels up in Heaven have a thousand things
                                        to do,
But there's one whose special interest is in little folks
                                        like you.
He watches out and gathers up the prayers of boys
                                        and girls,
And the name he has in Heaven is the Angel of the Pearls.

You may think it's nothing wonderful to kneel and say
                                        a prayer,
But every time you do it, there goes flashing through
                                        the air
A something bright and precious. See, the angel's fingers
                                        twirl
As he catches it and holds it up. Your prayer is now a
                                        pearl!

Oh, he's watching in the morning, and he's watching
                                        all the day,
And all the night he's watching out for every prayer
                                        you say.
He never, never misses one, so any boy or girl
From any place, at any time, can send him up a pearl.

He never gets too many and he welcomes every one,
And he gives it to Our Lady, who presents it to her Son.
(That makes it near and dear to Him) and then the boy
                                        or girl
Is blessed by God in Heaven for the prayer that's now
                                        a pearl.

The angel then goes over to a crown that's made to
                                        measure
To fit a certain little head, and next, with keenest pleasure,
He sets this latest pearl into your crown, and then he
                                        stands
In breathless admiration of the glory in his hands!

This angel is an expert and can tell as quick as thought
If pearls are good or only fair, and sometimes he has
                                        caught
An ugly, burnt-out cinder that could never, never pass;
You send no pearl to Heaven when you laugh or talk
                                        at Mass.

But prayers well said at Mass are what the angel loves
                                        to see,
And he loves the shining string of pearls we call a rosary;
And here's a little secret that keeps pearls from being dull:
A prayer that's said for souls in need is doubly beautiful.

Oh, the angels up in Heaven have a thousand things to do,
But there's one whose special interest is in little folks
                                        like you.
He gives to God, through Mary, all the prayers of boys
                                        and girls,
And 'twas Mother Mary christened him "the Angel of
                                        the Pearls!"

The Little Plaster Shepherd

Down in the basement where the crib is kept,
The little plaster statues through the long year slept.
The kings and the camels and the shepherds packed
                                            together
Slept through the spring and the hot summer weather;
Slept through the fall, till, far-off and dim,
The choir started practising a Christmas hymn.
That wakened up the statues, and: "How time goes!"
Said a little plaster shepherd with a broken nose.

He stretched out his arms and he poked a sleepy ox,
And wakened up the camels at the bottom of the box;
Helped a plaster king to find a crown he had mislaid,
Rummaged through the straw to find the flute he never
                                            played.
All began to talk and tried to figure out the date.
"I'll bet it's near the time, because that choir is always late.
I wonder what's been happening since we began to doze,"
Said the little plaster shepherd with the broken nose.

"I wonder if the people will be good this year;
I wonder where they'll put us and what kind of prayers
                                            we'll hear.
Will some be just as kindly, will some be just as cold?
Will some be just as crazy for pleasure, pride or gold?
Will some ask God for favours that would only serve
                                            them ill,
And then get mad and quit because God doesn't do
                                            their will?
Will some believe they're pious while they're hating all
                                            their foes?"
Said the little plaster shepherd with the broken nose.

"Others I'll be looking for — remember them last year?
The little folks who clustered round and made us want
                                    to cheer;
The weary folks, hungry folks, out-of-work and sad,
Who knelt to think of Bethlehem, and God made them glad;
The sinners — pretty tough they were — who came on
                                    Christmas Eve,
Said their penance near us and went humbly to receive.
The bunch of resolutions I overheard that night —
I'm wild to get some news of them, I'll bet they're coming
                                    right.
If not, we'll see them mended where the Star of Christmas
                                    glows,"
Said the little plaster shepherd with the broken nose.

Silence for a moment, then a sigh! ...And a king
Spoke softly through the straw: "Are you in need of
                                    anything?"
Said the little plaster shepherd: "I'm thinking of the places
Where young folk and old folk never see our faces:
Lands like yours, where there isn't any Star
To lead to where the Christ-Child and His Mother are.
Will no one ever bring us where the Yangtse flows?"
Asked the little plaster shepherd with the broken nose.

Down in the basement where the crib is kept,
The little plaster statues through the long year slept.
The kings and the camels and the shepherds packed
                                    together
Slept through the spring and the hot summer weather;
Slept through the fall, but now they arise
To paint their Christmas picture for your glistening eyes.
"And sad eyes are waiting where the Yangtse flows,"
Says the little plaster shepherd with the broken nose.

A Man Like Dad

I've been wondering what the saints were like,
When they lived on this earth like me.
How did they walk? And what did they do?
And what were they like to see?
What did they work at? How did they talk?
What were the cares they had?
And I've figured it out that in lots of things
One saint was a main like Dad.

St. Peter had eyebrows bushy and big,
And he ruled and travelled and taught;
St. Paul was smaller, but wiry and quick,
And many a fight he fought.
St. Francis, in brown, loved prayer and song,
And his keen face never was sad;
But St. Joseph, he was head of the house,
So he was a man like Dad.

St. Joseph, he had his trade and his shop,
His tools and his working clothes.
Oh, from Monday morning to Saturday night
The round of labour he knows:
The ache in the arms when the work piles high,
In the heart, when the times are bad,
And sweetness of Home when the day is done;
For he was a man like Dad.

St. Joseph sawed and hammered and planed
For food, for rent and for heat;
And the wrinkles came on his face with the years
Of trying to make ends meet.
His hands were hard and his back was stooped,
But precious the charge he had;
So he laboured on for a Mother and Child —
For he was a man like Dad.

St. Joseph, he hadn't a college degree;
There were books that he hadn't read.
But against his breast that was loving and kind
He pillowed a tired Child's head;
And his arm was strong for Our Lady's need;
Ah, great were the honours he had.
His lore and his wealth were a lowly Home —
Yes, he was a man like Dad.

I'm praying hard for a day to come,
When a few more years are past,
When the Child Whom St. Joseph bore in his arms
Will make me His priest at last.
When I stand that day at the altar steps,
In my priestly vestments clad,
St. Joseph (I'm sure) with a blessing will send
Congratulations to Dad!

"A Boy's Best Friend"

When Our Lord asked Our Lady to think of Saint John
As a child of her own, then His gaze travelled on
Over time, over distance, to far-away me
And He meant that His Mother my Mother should be.

When He died for mankind — died for all and each one,
She saw we were dearer than life to her Son:
He died to adopt everyone as His brother,
And that's why the Queen of All Saints is our Mother.

Gee, I wish I could tell it out just like I feel!
But see for yourself — go right up there and kneel
At her altar … You know, when the Wise Men came round
'Twas with Mary His Mother the Christ-Child was found.

It makes me feel good — just to know that God cares;
There He stays on the Altar to hear my old prayers,
And He gives me Himself! — and the Star of the Sea,
His Mother, my heavenly Mother to be.

And I know what a Mother can mean to a guy —
Gee, I'm fond of my Mum! — and therefore, think I,
If my Mother on earth's a sweet Mother Machree,
How lovely my heavenly Mother must be!

Parting Ways

He's the fellow I go to the movies with,
The fellow whose books I borrow,
The guy I've been playing and scrapping with,
And he's going away tomorrow.
He's the closest pal that I've ever had —
I've known him since I was four —
And now he's going to China, Dad,
And I'm — going into the store!

And he'll be out in China, a priest, a priest in China,
Baptizing folks in China, and I'll be in a store;
Saying Mass in China, with his chalice out in China,
While Saint Peter holds a crown for him inside of
Heaven's door.

We both had wheels, our routes were the same,
And in seventeen kinds of weather,
He with the *News* and I with the *Sun,*
We always rode together;
And the time I was bad in the hospital, Dad,
It was he who came to the door
To ask — but he's going to China now,
And I'm — going into a store!

We had it fixed that we'd both be cops
(We were only eight, you know),
Later we changed it to cowboy stars;
But that seems so long ago!

For we've said good-bye at the gym tonight,
And we'll scarcely meet any more,
For he'll be a priest in China, Dad,
And I'll be — a clerk in a store!

Oh, I've tried to pretend, but you've noticed, Dad,
I didn't seem happy, you said.
Well, there's something that comes, and it isn't the store,
And it won't stay out of my head.
It's something that Mother was praying about,
When she died, and for months before.
Oh, can I be a priest in China, Dad,
And — forget that job in the store?

And I'll be there in China — a priest, a priest in China,
Riding out in China with the pal I used to know,
Saying Mass, baptising, preaching, building,
                                        catechising,
Till we both ride Home together as we both rode long ago!